Taylor Alison Swift was born on December 13, 1989, in West Reading, Pennsylvania. Her parents named her after James Taylor, a famous musician.

A lot of love surrounded Taylor and her little brother, Austin. The Swifts did many activities as a family. They spent time reading books, visiting new places, and having fun outside.

TAYLOR SWIFT

A Little Golden Book® Biography

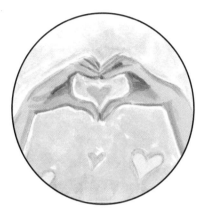

By Wendy Loggia

Illustrated by Elisa Chavarri

The author dedicates this book to her daughter, Olivia Joyce:
I always have the best day with you.

A GOLDEN BOOK • NEW YORK

Text copyright © 2023 by Wendy Loggia
Cover art and interior illustrations copyright © 2023 by Elisa Chavarri
All rights reserved. Published in the United States by Golden Books, an imprint of Random
House Children's Books, a division of Penguin Random House LLC, 1745 Broadway,
New York, NY 10019. Golden Books, A Golden Book, A Little Golden Book, the G colophon,
and the distinctive gold spine are registered trademarks of Penguin Random House LLC.
rhcbooks.com
Educators and librarians, for a variety of teaching tools, visit us at RHTeachersLibrarians.com
Library of Congress Control Number: 2022931984
ISBN 978-0-593-56671-8 (trade) — ISBN 978-0-593-56672-5 (ebook)
Printed in the United States of America
10 9

Christmas was one of Taylor's favorite holidays. And what made the holiday season even more exciting was that her family lived on a Christmas tree farm!

"I really love Christmas. I wish it was all year round."

Everyone pitched in at Christmastime. Taylor's dad mowed the fields on his tractor. Taylor's job? Picking praying mantis egg pods off the trees. The Swifts didn't want anyone to get a buggy surprise on Christmas morning!

As a kid, Taylor tried lots of different things. She rode horses. She acted in plays. She wrote poetry. But when she learned how to play the guitar, she knew she had found her passion.

When Taylor has a goal, nothing stops her!
She was a big fan of country superstars Faith
Hill and Shania Twain, and she discovered
that both musicians had started their careers
in Nashville, Tennessee.

That was all ten-year-old Taylor needed to know. She asked her parents to take her to Nashville. She asked them every day. And finally, when she was eleven, it happened! Her mom took Taylor and Austin there for spring break. They drove up and down Music Row—an area with country music recording studios and businesses. While Taylor's mom and brother waited in the car, Taylor ran into the offices of various record labels and handed out CDs she'd made of her music.

Taylor performed anywhere that would have her, including fairs, festivals, and ball games. But sometimes following dreams means doing things other people don't understand. Girls at school were mean to Taylor. Her classmates thought it was weird to like country music so much.

This made Taylor sad. But it didn't stop her from doing what she loved.

When Taylor was thirteen, something incredible happened. RCA Records wanted to work with her! Taylor and her family said goodbye to Pennsylvania and moved to Nashville. Her dream of being a country-music star was about to come true!

For Taylor, writing songs was just as important as singing them. But because she was young, the record company wanted her to sing other people's songs. And they thought she should wait until she was older before she made her own album.

Taylor didn't agree. One night, Taylor performed at Nashville's Bluebird Café. She sang some of her own songs and some songs from other singers. She caught the eye of a music executive in the crowd who was forming a new record label. Guess who he signed up to make an album? Taylor Swift!

Taylor's debut album, *Taylor Swift*, came out when she was just sixteen. She was excited every time she heard her songs on the radio! Her next album, *Fearless*, was the top-selling record of the year—and made Taylor a huge star.

Taylor *is* fearless. When she went on her first concert tour, she took the music world by storm!

One of Taylor's biggest strengths is storytelling—her songs tell stories that many people can relate to.

Taylor wrote all the songs on her third album, *Speak Now*. Listening to a Taylor Swift album is like hearing her diary being sung out loud!

Many of Taylor's songs are inspired by her life, like "The Best Day," a song about growing up in a loving family and having a supportive mom.

Taylor and her mom, Andrea, are very close. They talk about everything. No one has known Taylor longer—or knows her better—than her mom!

Trying new things and taking risks is important to Taylor. Even though country music was her first love, she took a big chance and recorded a pop album called *1989*—and it was the best-selling album of the year! Taylor never lets anything hold her back from creating music she loves.

Taylor also loves sharing things with her fans. They know that her lucky number is thirteen. She often hides clues and symbols in her music and videos. For a few of her albums, she surprised special groups of fans by inviting them to secret parties to listen to the album before anyone else. They got to hang out at her house, meet her family—and even bake cookies together!

When Taylor likes something, she tells everyone about it. One thing she really likes? Cats!

Taylor has a big reputation for speaking out against racial injustice and for encouraging people to vote. She stands up for other artists and herself, even when it's tough. She's not just a superstar—she's a trailblazer!

Taylor's hard work has paid off. Her albums have sold millions of copies. She has won multiple Grammys. She's traveled around the world and made people happy with her music. What will she do next?

When you're Taylor Swift, the sky's the limit!